Matilda went rushing into tl
today we are going to Penzan
she asked her mother feeling

"Yes, I have packed the case," her Mother replied, "so you must hurry and take Bracken for a walk after breakfast."

Matilda quickly had breakfast and then took Bracken to the local park for a walk. He was a beautiful black and white dog, and was her best friend. Her Mother had agreed that Bracken could go on holiday with them as he was no longer a puppy and Matilda had trained him to be very obedient.

They always had a family summer holiday, but her Father was away on business this year so it was just her Mother she was going with. They were staying in a small cottage outside Penzance which was near the beach and also had a garden for Bracken to play in.

"We are ready now," said her mother, when Matilda and Bracken returned from their walk. "I have a picnic to eat on the journey so we will now go to the railway station."

They set off down the road to the station and boarded the train. It was quite full as it was lovely weather and everybody seemed to be going on holiday.

They soon reached Penzance station and carried their case to a waiting taxi which took them to the cottage.

Matilda and her Mother unpacked their clothes and put them away in the tiny chest of drawers in the bedrooms. Matilda had a small room to herself at the front of the cottage overlooking the garden.

She changed into her jeans and fleecy top and then took Bracken into the garden to play ball before bedtime. Her mother stood by the garden fence watching.

It was soon time for bed as they were tired after the long train journey. Matilda's Mother made them some hot chocolate and buttered some scones for their supper. Matilda then took Bracken to their bedroom where he was soon curled up on his favourite blanket at the side of Matilda's bed.

When they awoke the next morning the sun was shining very brightly through the window.

After breakfast Matilda was eager to explore the beach, and her Mother decided to go with her. Matilda helped to carry her Mother's deckchair onto the beach where she sat to read her book.

Matilda and Bracken played with the ball for a while and then wandered over to the rocks. Sitting on the top of a rock was an octopus watching them and wishing he could join in.

Matilda saw a small boat the other side of the rocks and decided to have a look. She peeped inside and saw a mermaid lying in the bottom.

Bracken barked at her, and the mermaid was very frightened.

"Don't be afraid," said Matilda, as she knelt by the side of the boat, "Bracken will not harm you as he is very soft and gentle. What is your name and what are you doing in this boat?"

"My name is Myrtle," the mermaid replied, "I went for a swim but have come too far and am too tired to swim back. Can you help me?"

"Yes, I will row you back home," replied Matilda, and Bracken sat in the boat with them.

They rowed past the lighthouse and Matilda had to stop soon as she was becoming very tired. She was by some rocks and she climbed out onto a small patch of sand. She found an old piece of rope by a rock which she tied round the rock, and tied the other end to the boat.

Sitting on top of the rock was a seal, and Matilda started to climb towards it. Bracken would not follow her as he was frightened of the funny creature.

"You are a silly dog," said Matilda, "it will be quite safe, but you had better stay here with Myrtle, and wait for me."

"Do you live on this rock?" she asked the seal feeling a little scared as she approached him.

"Yes, and you should not be here," said the seal with a very strong deep voice, "this is my home and I don't like having visitors."

"I love my friends calling on me to play in my home," said Matilda, and she sat on a small rock near the seal. "What is your name?"

"I don't know what you mean by 'name'," said the seal looking puzzled at this little girl who had disturbed him.

"When you meet your friends what do they call you?" asked Matilda, beginning to feel sorry for the seal. "I don't have any friends and when somebody wants to speak to me they just call me 'seal'." he replied, "What do your friends call you?"

"My name is 'Matilda', and now we must think of a name for you. I know, we will call you 'Sandy Seal' as you live near a sandy beach," she shouted, clapping her hands and laughing.

"What are you doing here?" asked Sandy Seal, and he climbed slowly off the rock.

"I am rowing a mermaid back to her home, but am finding it very hard work," replied Matilda. She turned to Myrtle who had stayed in the boat with Bracken and introduced her to Sandy Seal. "Could you please help with the rowing?" she asked.

"I would be glad to help," he replied feeling very pleased that he had a name and some friends.

They all got into the boat and Sandy Seal rowed round to a small cove where he stopped by a beach.

"I am finding this hard work and I know a crab lives near in a rock pool so we could ask him to help," he said as he pulled the boat onto the beach.

Matilda and the seal went in search of the crab, leaving Bracken behind as he was still frightened. He stayed by the boat holding the rope in his mouth to make sure it did not float away.

They found the crab enjoying himself splashing around in his rock pool.

"What are you doing near my pool and why is that seal here?" bellowed the crab.

"He is our friend," said Matilda stepping away from the not so friendly crab. "What is your name?"

"What do you mean by 'name'?" asked the crab.

"What do your friends call you when you meet them?" asked Matilda.

"I don't have any friends," replied the crab looking sad, "and when anybody wants to speak to me they just call me 'crab'. What do your friends call you?"

"My name is Matilda and this is Sandy Seal," she said, "and now we must think of a name for you."

She thought very hard for a few minutes, and then shouted, "We will call you 'Charlie Crab'."

"Thank you, I like that name very much," said Charlie Crab smiling.

Sandy Seal and Charlie Crab began chatting away as if they had been friends for years.

"We wondered if you could help us to row a mermaid back to her home?" asked Matilda when she could get a word in as they were talking so much.

"Yes," they said together, and then they giggled like children. "I will be very happy to help the mermaid," said Charlie Crab as he was introduced to her.

So they all got into the boat and Charlie Crab began rowing. "I am getting tired and do not think I can go much further," he said after a while, and had to stop near some rocks. "I know a lobster lives in a shipwreck near here and he may be able to help us."

"Well let us go and visit him, and you can tell him your names, and ask if he can help," said Matilda.

"He is not a friendly lobster," said Sandy Seal, "and is sometimes quite cross."

They all got out of the boat, and left Bracken to guard it while they found the shipwreck.

They soon found the lobster and he was very big and angry.

"What do you want and what are you doing near my home?" he shouted.

"We want to tell you our names," said Sandy Seal, not put off by the grumpy lobster. "I am Sandy Seal and crab is now called Charlie Crab. We are good friends and wondered if you would like a name too."

"What is a name?" asked the lobster. "And why do I need one?

"It is what people call you when they want to speak to you instead of just 'lobster'," said Charlie Crab.

"I think we shall name you 'Larry Lobster' as it sounds very grand," said Matilda.

"I like it," cried Larry Lobster, with a big smile.

"We are helping a mermaid to go home, and would like some help to row the boat," said Matilda. "Could you help us?"

"I would love to help with the rowing," said Larry Lobster, "but first you must have a drink."

Myrtle was introduced to Larry Lobster, and they all sat on the sand to have a lovely cool drink made from seaweed. They chatted away as if they had known each other for years.

"Now I am ready to do some rowing for you," said Larry Lobster, and they all settled down in the boat.

After about twenty minutes Larry Lobster was struggling to keep up with rowing and had to stop.

"Oh dear me I need to rest," he sighed, "I cannot go any further."

"Do you know of anyone else who can help us?" asked Matilda thinking they were never going to get Myrtle Mermaid home.

"Yes, I know where a turtle lives," replied Larry Lobster, "and I think I can manage to row there.

He rowed them to a tiny fishing harbour where a turtle lived in a cave.

"This is where the turtle lives," he said, getting out of the boat and disappearing into the cave. He soon reappeared with a turtle following him.

"I am very busy," said the turtle as he joined everyone by the boat. "What do you want?"

"We want to tell you our names," said Charlie Crab, "and to ask if you would like one."

"What is a name?" asked the turtle, "And why would I want one?"

"It is what people call you when they want to speak to you, and Matilda will give you one like she did for us," said Sandy Seal.

"I think we will name you Terry Turtle," said Matilda.

"I like that name," said Terry Turtle, "now what can I do for you?"

"We need some help to row a mermaid round to her home," said Matilda, "and hoped you could do some rowing for us."

Terry Turtle, who was very strong, agreed to help and he soon had them all at the mermaid's home.

"Thank you all very much," she said, getting out of the boat. "I don't know how I would have managed without your kindness."

"There is no need to thank us," said Matilda, "it has been a lovely day out, but now I must get Bracken back to Penzance for tea as my Mother will be wondering what has happened to us."

Myrtle sat on the sand leaning by a rock as she was very tired, and watched her new friends disappear into the distance.

"I am too tired to row back," said Sandy Seal.

"So am I," said Terry Turtle.

"Me too," said Charlie Crab.

"I can row us to where a shark lives who may help," said Larry Lobster.

"He is a nasty shark," said Sandy Seal, "but if we all stick together then he cannot harm us."

"I will soon sort him out," said Matilda, but she felt a little bit nervous as she had heard people talk about sharks not being very friendly.

They rowed round to a small island where Sandy Seal thought the shark lived.

They all climbed out of the boat and were glad of a rest from rowing. Matilda walked into a very large cave with the others not far behind her. As usual Bracken had stayed outside with the boat.

Suddenly there was a roar and a large angry shark came into the cave with Bracken in his mouth.

"I found this creature on a patch of sand by a boat and I want to know what he is doing here," bellowed the shark as Bracken fell out of his mouth and landed on the floor of the cave with a thump.

Matilda could see the shark was not very happy at finding a dog near his home.

"What have you done to my dog?" cried Matilda as she put her arms round Bracken's neck and stroked him. "You are a big bully, and I don't think I want to give you a name."

"What is a name?" bellowed the shark. "And why should I need one?"

"It is what other people call you when they want to speak to you instead of just 'shark'," said Larry Lobster suddenly feeling brave, "but because you have been nasty to Matilda's dog I don't think you deserve one."

The shark went very quiet. "I would really like to have a name," he said, "I am not happy at being called 'shark'."

"I shall have to think very hard to decide on a name for you," said Matilda, "and when I give you a name you must be nice and friendly to everybody else who lives here."

"Oh please give me a name, and I will be kind and friendly to everybody," said the shark.

"You shall be known as Shaun Shark," Matilda decided, "and now you must be nice to Bracken."

Shaun Shark went to Bracken who was shaking with fright, and picked him up and placed him on Sandy Seal's back. "You can have a ride back to the boat," he said.

"Yes we must be going back to the beach as my Mother will be wondering what has happened to us," said Matilda, "but we are all too tired after rowing from Penzance and we wondered if you could help us get back."

"I would be pleased to help and I can push the boat with you all in it," said Shaun Shark as he lifted Bracken off Sandy Seal's back and placed him in the boat.

So Shaun Shark pushed the boat back round the coast to Penzance and onto the beach where Matilda had left her Mother reading in the deckchair.

Matilda was feeling sad at leaving her new friends. "You must keep in touch with each other," she said as she and Bracken climbed out of the boat.

"We will keep in touch," said Shaun Shark, "and we must thank you for bringing us all together and giving us names."

Matilda suddenly felt a cold wet nose on her face, and she opened her eyes. She was lying in the boat and Bracken was licking her face. He was getting fed up with being on his own.

"Oh, where am I?" as she realised she had fallen asleep in the bottom of the boat. "I must have been dreaming," she said to Bracken and stroked his fur. It was very wet. "Could I have dreamt it?" she thought, very puzzled.

They set off back to where her Mother was sitting in the deckchair.

"Have you had a nice time playing on the beach?" asked her Mother, "You both seem to be quite wet. What have you been up to?"

"We rowed a mermaid named Myrtle round to her home and we met some very nice sea creatures on our journey," replied Matilda, thinking that her Mother would not believe her and she was right.

"You must have been dreaming," cried her Mother in astonishment. "How can you talk to these sea creatures?" and she laughed until tears were running down her cheeks.

Matilda didn't know what to say or do to make her Mother believe her, and she was beginning to think she had dreamt it all.

It was then that Bracken started to bark and wag his tail as he looked out to sea. Matilda looked and saw all the sea creatures on some rocks by the lighthouse watching as if they were saying goodbye.

Matilda's Mother had to believe their story when she saw the shark leaping about.

She stood with Matilda and Bracken, and they all waved. She was a little sorry she had missed the 'seaside adventure'.

They then walked back to the cottage and forgot about the deckchair and book which had fallen onto the sand.

This was a good thing as the octopus was sitting in the deckchair watching them walk away.

THE END

All rights reserved. No part of this publication may be reproduced, converted or archived into any other medium without the relevant permission first being obtained from the publisher. Nor should the book be circulated or resold in any binding other than its original cover.

Matilda's Seaside Adventure

Story & Illustrations © Joan Power

First Edition published 2017

Printed & Published by:

St Ives Printing & Publishing Company,
High Street, St Ives, Cornwall TR26 1RS, UK

www.stivesworldwide.co.uk

ISBN: 978-0-948385-85-8